Free to Live

Create a Thriving Unschooling Home

PAM LARICCHIA

Published by
Living Joyfully Enterprises
Erin, Ontario, Canada

ISBN: 978-0-9877333-4-4

Edited by Alexandra Peace.

Cover design by Jane Dixon-Smith.

Cover photo by Lissy Laricchia.

I dedicate this book to the wonderful unschooling parents who, over the last decade, have spent a significant amount of their online time sharing their family's unschooling experiences, helping me and countless others on our unschooling journeys. They are a big part of the reason why my relationships with my children are so strong and for that I am intensely grateful.

Contents

What you'll find in *Free to Live*

Introduction

The Trait of Curiosity

Curiosity is the spark that drives us to explore and learn. Why is that important for unschooling?

The Trait of Patience

Patience helps us move at our child's pace. When our children are interested in something, we, as best we can, should meet them where they are. Trying to rush someone else's learning doesn't actually make it happen any faster. In fact, it can slow it down.

The Power of Strong Relationships

The development and maintenance of strong connections between parents and children so that both are comfortable approaching each other is fundamental to a nurturing unschooling environment.

Cultivating Trust

Trust grows with experience and helps us move more courageously into the future, through our fear of the unknown.

It allows you and your children to live together more openly, better understanding situations because you are both more comfortable sharing your perspectives.

Introduction

Hi, I'm Pam Laricchia. I thought I'd share a bit about my journey to unschooling. Our family—myself and my husband Rocco, along with our three children, Joseph, Lissy, and Michael—has been unschooling in Ontario, Canada since 2002. That's when I discovered homeschooling (and soon after, unschooling) and the kids happily took us up on our offer to stay home to learn.

My backstory includes a successful academic career, earning an Engineering and Management bachelor's degree through a unique five-year university program. I found an interesting job, married the terrific man I met at a summer job during my university career, and we had our three children over the next five years. It has always been in my nature to question things that don't seem to make sense in my world, but even as my parenting began veering from the mainstream, it didn't occur to me to question the school system when my eldest reached school age. I do remember thinking it would be an interesting ride when we walked out of Joseph's junior kindergarten teacher interview, during which he didn't say a word to answer her questions. He smiled and explained to me that he didn't feel like talking to her today, but that he'd speak to her once he started school. I laughed and tousled his hair.

In those first years some teachers were more flexible, while others were quite determined to shave off his uniqueness. I researched, I left my career to stay home full-time, and I worked with his teachers and principals to try to help them better understand him. I even gave a presentation about spirited kids at a teacher's meeting and donated books to the library for other parents. Most of the teachers understood what I was talking about, but their feedback was that they don't have the time to work with kids outside the personalities and learning styles that mesh with the classroom setting. The kids have to fit the surroundings, not the other way around. It became clear to me that he would not thrive in public school. In my continued quest to find a learning environment that worked well for him, I found a specialized private school. The environment was better—the teachers and staff were being paid to work outside the typical lines—but still not great.

Then, through still more research, I came across the concept of homeschooling and was thrilled to discover it was legal in Canada. Rocco and I discussed it at length over the next couple of weeks and realized that there seemed no downside to trying it out for a year; if it didn't work out they could return to school. It was March Break and none of the kids went back. They were ecstatic with their newly-found playtime and I was now happily researching homeschooling. I soon discovered the notion of unschooling and after a couple weeks of trying to entice them to do some workbooks, I realized I was hindering, not helping, their learning. We spent the next months deschooling and living and having a great time. Eventually I realized we were truly unschooling and we haven't looked back since!

A *Free to Learn* Primer

My first book, *Free to Learn*, is about the five ideas, and resulting paradigm shifts, I found most helpful as I learned about unschooling. It's more than just not going to school—unschooling is about creating a different kind of learning environment. I have included a quick synopsis here because I think it's important to have a good understanding of the principles behind unschooling before tackling this book. *Free to Learn* helps you understand what unschooling is and why you might want your children to learn in this way, whereas *Free to Live* digs into the details of how to create a thriving unschooling environment. Life can flow more smoothly when you understand your goal before figuring out how to reach it.

The first idea, or unschooling principle, discussed in *Free to Learn* is that learning is best defined by the learner. Instead of looking at learning from the teacher's point of view, it's more accurate to look at it from the learner's point of view. Real learning, learning that is understood and remembered, is best defined by the learner precisely because it can only take place in the learner, regardless of any teaching being done *around* the learner. If you find yourself using or thinking the word *teach*, take a moment to rethink the situation and substitute the word *learn*.

The second principle is that learning is found everywhere. Though many educational experts espouse the idea that they should define what, when, how, and where children learn, unschoolers shift that paradigm. Learning need not be defined as exclusively occurring in classrooms, during school hours, with those of school age; it can be found everywhere, at anytime, and can happen at any age. With this in mind, watch your kids as they play and you'll soon see so much learning.

The third unschooling principle is that choices are the key to learning. Parents who make most of the decisions for their child growing up are eager to model the "right" thing to do so that their children will remember and make those same choices as young adults and beyond. But instead of learning *what* choices to make, isn't it better to learn *how* to make informed choices? That way they are better equipped to deal with new situations as they arise.

The fourth idea is "why not yes?" We often hear the message that it's important for parents to set boundaries for their children, and a definitive *no* helps the parents stay in control. Sure, saying no can make life seem easier in the moment, but saying yes encourages children to explore their world and cultivates their ability to live confidently in it. Take a moment to ask yourself if that automatic no is really necessary.

The fifth unschooling principle is that kids are people too. It can seem like parents have, by virtue of age and childbirth, earned a position of power, but everyone in the family has important needs and wants and can have a voice, without it leading to chaos.

If any of those ideas left you puzzled, I'd recommend reading *Free to Learn* before you dig into the ideas in this book. Otherwise you might just end up feeling even more flummoxed!

Will Unschooling Work for My Child?

If the principles behind unschooling make sense to you, the next step is to consider whether this learning lifestyle is something you want to pursue with your own family. At this point parents often ask, "Will unschooling work for *my* child?"

The short, and truthful, answer to this question is an emphatic *yes*. Unschooling, done well, will work for any child. It's tailored to the child's interests, needs, and personality after all. But what most questioners don't yet realize is that this is not the question they should be asking to figure out if unschooling will work well in their family. What they should really be asking is, "Will *I* be able to unschool my child?"

Do you see the distinction? It's a subtle but very important difference that speaks to the point of view of the question. It is the *parents'* responsibility to cultivate the learning environment for the child, not the child's responsibility to figure out how unschooling will work best for them.

This shift is similar to the shift of focus from teaching to learning I mentioned earlier: parents and/or teachers can do all sorts of teaching around the child, but any learning happens in the child—it is their choice. With the wording "will unschooling work for my child?" the focus is subtly but surely on the child fitting into unschooling. With "will I be able to unschool my child?" the focus is instead on the parent setting up unschooling effectively for the child. That's the right perspective. With unschooling, parents are choosing to have their children's learning foundation be based at home rather than at school, and are therefore choosing to take on that responsibility rather than hand it over to the school system.

Why is the parents' contribution so critical? Because with unschooling there is not a set of rules or curriculum that parents can take and mechanically implement in their family to guarantee unschooling will work well. Instead, parents need to understand the unschooling principles about learning and combine that with their understanding of their unique children and family dynamic to create a thriving unschooling environment in their home—whatever that looks like day-to-day.

I think now would be a good time to remember that choosing school's learning environment and curriculum is no guarantee of success either, though it can be comforting to pass the responsibility (and potential blame) to others. But ultimately, whether choosing public, private, alternative, or home-based schooling, the children's learning environment is the parents' responsibility.

The parents have chosen unschooling as the way their children will learn, so it's not surprising that it's the efforts of the *parents* that are important to the question of unschooling. If the parents create an environment that truly supports their child's individuality, unschooling will work well for any child.

Learning about Living

In *Free to Live* I'll be discussing four key characteristics of a thriving unschooling home—whether home is a building, an RV, or a boat. There are a number of family characteristics that allow learning to flourish, but the four I'll discuss here are those that, in my experience, have made the most positive impact on our unschooling lifestyle. When they're absent, I don't think unschooling will work as well as it could—or at least it becomes more challenging for the child to blossom.

But not to worry, these characteristics can be developed. Understanding *why* they are so helpful to unschooling is a first step and can be a key motivator. It's so much easier to cultivate these characteristics when you can see the big picture rooted in that small moment. With that understanding, it is easier for a parent to choose to respond in ways that support unschooling, rather than ways that undermine it.

And as I emphasized in *Free to Learn*, as you're reading, don't just skim through the ideas, as logical as they may seem on the surface. Really live with them. Let them percolate in the back of your mind as you go about your day. Recall your own learning experiences, your own childhood and relationships with your parents, and see how they compare. Not in long, retreat-type hours set aside for the purpose of self-reflection, but in smaller snippets as they appear during your days.

That's the interesting thing about real learning. You can read about stuff, it can make sense to you intellectually, but until you've made it personal, it still just sits on the surface. Me, you, each of us individually need to do this work for ourselves, this learning about unschooling. *That* is where we make our own connections, where we build our own real learning. Knowledge we understand so deeply that we can make connections from it to the new places our family will go. When next month brings a new twist, we can call on our understanding of the underlying principles of unschooling, overlay it onto this new situation, and make the intuitive leaps and connections that will point us to a path forward that will be helpful and supportive of our unique family, rather than being caught in the confusion of the unknown, wondering what a mythical "perfect" unschooling parent would do.

Your learning is the key. My intention with this book is to walk with you, sharing my thoughts and my experience, inspiring you to add your own experiences and observations to the mix and eventually draw your own conclusions. It will take work on your part to deeply understand these concepts and bring them into the everyday life of your family, but it will be truly rewarding.

The Trait of Curiosity

I've found that one of the key characteristics of a thriving unschooling home is curiosity. Curiosity is the spark that drives us to explore. Unschooling won't work as well as it could if the parents aren't curious about the world around them.

Inquisitive parents are beautiful examples of some of the main ideas behind unschooling:

- that pursuing what catches your interest leads to fun and rewarding days;
- that all sorts of learning happens alongside that pursuit of fun; and
- that exploring and learning is a lifelong adventure, not just the domain of the young.

Unschooling works better when the parents dive into the lifestyle instead of expectantly waiting for their children to discover the joys of learning themselves.

Curiosity versus Curriculum

"Mrs. Appleby, what happens if the denominator isn't the same for all the fractions? How do you add them together then?" "You don't need to know that now, Olivia, you'll learn that next year."

Outside the school environment, the timeline of learning defined by curriculum is artificial. It's really only required by school's need to teach a fixed amount of information, to a large number of students, over a certain period of time. While both schooling and unschooling have a shared goal in helping children grow up able to live in the world as an adult, they take widely disparate paths to get there.

Compulsory schooling takes the path of teaching students generalized curricula, covering what the developers believe a typical person would need to know and, after graduation, judges them capable of living in the real world. In contrast, unschooling chooses living in the real world from the outset with each child learning what they, as unique individuals, encounter a need to know, and when.

Unschooling flips the curriculum model upside down in a number of ways:

- by appreciating that real learning is an improvement on the memorization valued by schools;

- by recognizing that the pattern of learning is rarely clean and linear, as a curriculum would imply, but messy and fun and unique to each individual; and
- by focusing on the lifelong nature of learning, of learning information and skills when an interest or need is encountered, regardless of age.

But without curricula to follow, how will children choose what to learn? By following their interests, their curiosity. Watch your children in action for a while and you will see them learning in leaps and bounds. Soon the idea of learning through following their interests won't seem so whimsical. But, if your children don't see *you* exploring the world alongside them, it becomes more difficult for them to discover that key relationship between living and learning: that learning something new is inexorably connected to a person's interest and need, not their age.

As parents creating an unschooling environment, why is that a key notion for our children to pick up? And by pick up I don't mean ensure they are *taught* it, but that they are immersed in it, living it, *learning* it. It's important because it demonstrates to them how learning is driven by curiosity, not age-dependent curriculum.

Real learning, learning that is understood and remembered (not memorized and soon forgotten), happens best when the learner is fully engaged, immersed in the activity at hand. And that happens when they are driven by an interest or need to get to the other side: understanding. Learning can be seen as a by-product—knowledge or skill picked up along the way to reaching their real goal. Real learning connects new knowledge in some way, through interest or need, to the person's current understanding of the world—this connection expands their understanding, and this new bigger picture makes sense, helping them remember it. It helps them reach their goal.

Without glowing examples of curiosity and determination close at hand, unschooling children may not develop the drive to explore the things they discover around them, or the tenacity to choose a goal and grab on. This is the drive to learn. Curiosity is, in essence, the replacement for curriculum when unschooling. And that is why being curious is such an important trait for unschooling parents to embrace.

Apathy Keeps the World Small

"Look at the Lego tower I built!" James pulls you by the hand into the living room to show off his creation. "That's cool, James." You smile and turn to leave. "Bill has a huge Lego spaceship! I'd love to build it too, can we get it?" His smile falters with your reply, "Maybe for your birthday." "But that's months away." Then his face brightens. "Oh! There's a Lego show at the Science Centre next week! Can we go?" "I don't think so, James, that's an hour drive away." Sighing, James turns back to his tower and attempts to add one more layer with his last few Lego pieces.

To dig further into our understanding of the link between curiosity and unschooling, let's peer into the future and speculate about what might happen down the road if unschooling parents aren't all that curious about life. Maybe they aren't drawn to delving into learning with their children for extended periods of time, they aren't taking their children out to explore the world, or bringing pieces of it home to share. In this case, the world, as seen by the children, is small. There isn't much around them to explore, and nobody around them seems very excited in doing so. Their curiosity is being dulled.

In this environment they may not develop the drive to explore the things they discover around them because there really isn't much that is interesting enough to catch their attention. If there aren't people in their lives showing them by example that learning is interesting and rewarding and fun, they may not discover the joy of learning. Seeing curious learners around them digging into a passing interest and discovering even more exciting connections than first anticipated, finding more fascinating pieces of the world, shows them the real value of curiosity. It motivates them to continue digging into their own interests to see what gold they may uncover.

It's true that they might discover that excitement on their own, coming across a passionate interest they are drawn to exploring, discovering the excitement that learning brings to their lives and taking that understanding into their next interest, but I'm not talking about leaving that to chance; I'm talking about creating a solid unschooling learning environment, not a wishy-washy one.

Let's look at this situation from the children's point of view: living in this environment may give them the impression that adult life is rather stagnant. Their parents aren't vigorously exploring life: they choose routine more often than spontaneous exploration; relaxed comfort more often than inquisitiveness; a tidy home over one with ongoing projects scattered about. And, as the kids get older they will also be picking up messages from the world around them: TV shows, books, movies, friends, and other adults in their lives.

What are some of the common messages about knowledge and learning? Children need to be taught; parents are always right; children should do what they're told without discussion; parents know everything; it's a child's job to go to school to learn; children will be accepted into the real world of grown-ups once they graduate etc.

Those messages won't mean much to an unschooling child if their personal experiences show them differently. In a curious and intellectually active family, those messages are likely to be springboards to interesting conversations about other parenting paradigms. And in contrast to those paradigms, they see their own parents open to discussion, changing their opinions as more information comes to light, learning new things far past graduation age, and enjoying that learning. In this situation, an unschooling child's personal observations lead them to see learning as something *anyone* can do, not just as a "child's job."

But, if those more mainstream messages line up with the child's own observations and experience, if their own parents aren't exploring and analyzing and learning in their day-to-day life, the child will begin to absorb those messages as truths. They may well build an understanding that adults don't spend much time learning new things, so they must indeed already know most everything they need to know, leading to the logical conclusion that most learning must therefore be done before they reach adulthood. In that situation, they may reach their teens, compare themselves to schooled kids, worry that they are behind, and blame unschooling, "Why didn't you make me learn that?"

Being curious and living a learning lifestyle right alongside your children can help them develop an understanding of how real learning is connected to the interesting things around them, and that age is irrelevant to this relationship. If they understand this intrinsically because it is their life experience (meaning, I wouldn't expect them to be able to explain, just live it), why would they ask their parent a question like "Why didn't you make me learn that?" Intuitively understanding the entangled nature of living and learning, if they encountered something they didn't yet know, they would be more likely to ask themselves if they are interested in pursuing it and, if the answer is yes, to go ahead and dive in. The question itself shows that the child still believes the choice of what to learn lies with adults, not with themselves; that they believe there is an age before which certain things should be known; and that they can't learn them today.

The young teen years can be challenging. Their schooled friends are likely looking forward to high school, excited to experience greater freedom than they've had before, both in the school structure and the possible increase in anonymity as the student body size grows. They imagine feeling more powerful because our ageist culture glorifies adults, and high school is a tangible symbol of their progress to adulthood. It is an exciting time in their lives for many of them, so it's understandable that they share this excitement with everyone around them, for many preceding months.

And their talk about classes at this age can sound so impressive: math equations, English essays, history projects, and science experiments. Eventually the excitement dies down as they discover it's still the same curriculum-driven cycle of homework, memorize, regurgitate, and move on—rinse and repeat. But in the meantime, in their excitement, they repeatedly express disbelief that their homeschooling friend wouldn't be thrilled to join them, "Now school's going to be fun!"

This is also a time when an unschooling child may be feeling unsettled and introspective as they ponder the transition from a child to a teen. They may find their enthusiasm for childhood loves waning, while at the same time still be casting about for new passions to catch their interest. An internalized understanding of the joy of learning, of heroically digging into connections, of following those threads as determinedly as Theseus did in the labyrinth, can help them be patient with themselves as they search for new interests. They intuitively know the learning process, how much fun it can be, even as it is challenging—they are just casting about for a topic or two upon which to apply it and dig in. Without the intrinsic awareness that learning can be found anywhere and pursued at any time to support them through the sometimes burdensome feeling of the responsibility for having control over their actions each and every day, the call of school can be quite strong: "They'll tell me what to do! Then I won't have to think for myself!"

This is not to judge choosing school as a "bad" choice. The main point is that it is a *choice*. And in choosing school they may well learn a lot. Not necessarily about the curriculum being presented or about curiosity and the lifelong nature of learning itself, but about themselves: the ways they enjoy learning, whether they are comfortable in that type of environment, etc. It can definitely be a learning experience, but school's strength isn't in demonstrating the *how* of real, deep, connected and joyful learning, its strength lies more in the business of moving large numbers of students through the various curricula.

So, we've been talking about how if unschooling parents aren't embracing their curiosity to explore the world, their kids may conclude that most learning needs to be done in childhood, and thus begin to feel shortchanged by their unschooling experience as they enter their teens, since unschooling is really about lifelong learning: learn it when you encounter a need or want for it, not because you're fourteen.

Being curious illustrates the beauty of digging into things. As an unschooling parent, do you struggle with finding and following your curiosity? The excitement of curiosity is in not knowing where something may lead, but knowing how interesting it is to find out. If you're feeling uninspired, how might you cultivate and share this curiosity about the world with your children?

Developing Curiosity

My daughter Lissy's answer to someone on her 365 photography project blog is an example of the deeper understanding about living and learning that curiosity can bring.

> *Anonymous asked*: Since you're unschooled do you plan on being a photographer for living? If you hadn't discovered photography what would you have done when you grew up? I've never heard of unschooled before.
>
> *Lissy replied*: That's the dream. I'm sure I would have discovered something else. Even those in school scarcely know what they want to do with the rest of their life, I'm lucky that even if I haven't found what I'm going to do for the rest of mine, I have something so fulfilling to fill the void.

Her reply shows her certainty that she would have discovered something else if photography didn't catch her passionate interest. And her belief that, in the future, if her interest in one thing wanes, there will be other interests that grow.

Now I didn't set out to "make sure she understands how interesting life is when one is curious." How might she have absorbed this? By seeing it play out time after time, not only in her own life, but in the lives of her siblings and parents. How following connections, being curious about where they might lead, time and again paid off in exciting, fun, and unexpected, ways.

How might parents show curiosity? There are a couple of key ways. First, when your child is interested in something, explore it with them! Be available when they want you with them. If you often prioritize other things over exploration, what message does that send? Show them with your actions that following their curiosity is a priority, and that it's fun and rewarding. If finding out the exact weight of a certain Pokémon isn't personally interesting to you, look at it through your child's eyes. See how interesting it is for them and share *that* excitement. Revel in *their* joy. Help them find the answer so they experience the satisfaction of a question laid to rest, and the gift of new questions appearing on their horizon. Follow the connections. And remember, by responding to their enthusiasm, you are encouraging them to continue bringing their interests to you in the future. Maybe the next one will be even more exciting!

And, certainly when they're younger, they may not know all the avenues of investigation that are available to them so be their guide. Find and share fun things that are connected to their interest: related TV shows or movies, museum or science centre exhibits, hands-on activity or quiet contemplation, books or magazines, toys or games, websites or blogs, forest walks or lake swims.

But as always, don't get so attached to these opportunities that you develop expectations of their response. Instead, take the stance that you are learning more about your children based on what connections *they* find interesting and want to pursue—you gain whether they say yes or no. You're still, and always, learning more about them, even if they don't want to pursue any of your suggestions right now. Over time you may come to see that the suggestion of yours that they chose not to pursue wasn't actually related to the central interest in their web of learning, but just a passing connection. Now their actions make more sense.

Your curiosity about your child's curiosity will help you learn so much about their lives; their interests, their likes and dislikes, and all the whys behind them. And it's that deeper understanding that will inform your actions and reactions moving forward: the things you will choose to point out to them; the things you will choose to sweep out of their way; the comments you will try to remember to share when they next pass through the room and those you'll make the trip to find them to share immediately; the places you will choose to take them and those you'll talk with them about waiting for the next opportunity. And if their reaction is different than you expected, it's not personal; it's just another piece of information for you about how they see the world.

Over time, your ability to help your children explore their interests will improve. Each time you see which threads they choose to follow and which they leave dangling, you learn a bit more about how they like to learn. And that corresponds with the ways they learn most effectively. But remember, people change. Don't cut off bits of the world forever; it makes it smaller. Our interests change over time, our point of view changes with experience, and our needs change as we get older. Those things that we passed on last year or last decade or last month might now make inspiring connections to our ever-evolving perspective.

Another way to model curiosity about life and learning is to have and explore your own interests, and to share those interests with your family. It doesn't need to be a big production, especially when the kids are younger and stretches of time on your own are few and far between. Maybe you like to read or knit and you do a bit sitting by them as they play, commenting with pleasure when you've found a new book or pattern. Or you enjoy making jewelry or duct tape wallets and you make space for their projects alongside yours. Maybe you've picked up a hula hoop or remote control plane that you've always thought might be fun and ask if they want to come outside too. Whatever your passion—invite them along. Even just reminding yourself why you do the day-to-day things that you do. Remembering the larger goal of your daily tasks can help put a bounce in your step. Think about new ways you might do them and share what you're thinking. Be curious.

A new way to organize the kitchen cupboards? Share your satisfaction! And it's so much easier to do when most of your pots and pans are already on the floor from their early morning game of "How fast can we empty the cupboard?"

A new place to fold laundry? "Come lie on the bed and I'll cover you in warm, fresh clothes." Then maybe together you rearrange their drawers so they can reach their t-shirts and choose their top each morning. Or grab a new one after a juice spill. Life is more fun for them, and a bit easier for you.

When the kids are older, your curiosity and explorations will probably look more purposeful. In our home it can look like my husband spending the day researching a new backup process for our network then working with each of us to set it up on our computers, or me reading about self-publishing and sharing some newfound insight about the industry over dinner. Or someone wandering out of their bedroom earlier in the morning than usual and seeing me doing some yoga. Living and learning together.

Without curious parents as examples of lifelong learning, developing a deep curiosity about the world around them can be challenging for children. We've talked about the messages that kids might pick up in that situation, but what might life look like from the parents' perspective if their kids haven't discovered the delight of curiosity? Life probably feels ho-hum, days become weeks become months. The kids do the same things they did the day before, and the day before that. Without the support of curious parents, they really haven't discovered that new things can become more interesting things, so unless something jumps out and grabs their full attention right away, they let it pass by. The parents might eventually come to question why their child doesn't seem interested in much of anything; they seem to just do the same thing over and over, maybe claiming that they are bored. That may lead the parents to start questioning unschooling: "I keep hearing about unschooling kids with passions and busy, interesting lives. Why isn't my child like that?"

When nagging questions begin to pester you, that's a good indicator that it's time to step things up, to look more deeply at situations and figure out why you're feeling uncomfortable. You're curious about what's going on with your child, right? So don't just observe *what* your child is doing; dig into the *why*. Not by asking directly, that will likely give away your discomfort with the situation, but by observing more closely. If your child is watching a lot of TV, watch it with them! And watch them. What things catch their attention? What do they react to? Talk with them about the shows themselves and listen to what they're thinking. There's a good chance they'll be happy to have you there and to share their thoughts.

Are they watching TV shows with curiosity and intention? Are they catching new nuances in the actors' (or voice actors') performances with each viewing? Or further memorizing the dialogue? Or gaining a deeper appreciation for the director's choices? Or relaxing with a loved and familiar show while processing unrelated stuff? Or do they seem bored? Is there a lack of other choices? Or a general lack of interest in pursuing other opportunities?

Let what you learn help you dig further and chances are eventually you'll discover the enjoyment and learning they are experiencing. You'll find they *do* have an interest, you were just not seeing the signs. Celebrate this with them! Find other things by their favourite directors, or find more information about the process voice actors use to record their dialogue—support and extend whatever it is that is catching their attention. If you discover that their extended time in front of the TV is more of a cocooning phase, needed to process other things, then bring them food and drinks, watch with them, make the spot extra comfortable. Be open and available to talk about anything that comes up: the TV shows, the experiences they are processing (if they want to), your experiences with relaxing (share your favourite comfort shows as a child, and now) and so on.

If you think that they are choosing TV more as a default, step up your interaction with the world. Offer things to do more often, but remember to offer things you think they might truly be interested in doing, not things you wish they were interested in doing. See the difference? And bring bits of the world to them: if you're out on an errand, bring them home a small surprise: a reading or activity book; a toy from their favourite show or a logic puzzle or a video game or a movie. Things they can enjoy right in the comfy spot they are sitting. Or a hula hoop or a jump rope if you think they'd like to move about. Or maybe look online for something they might enjoy without leaving their nest: free games; virtual museum tours or frog dissections; NASA space simulations; basic game development programs; a new recipe for you to bake. So many possibilities!

The point is, if you're feeling discomfort when you're unschooling, don't ignore it. It's good to question the unschooling environment you're creating from time to time (though if you're feeling discomfort often, you probably need to start asking yourself bigger questions about unschooling than just the environment you are creating). It's a great time to check that you've not lost your curiosity about life, that you're fully supporting their explorations, and making their world bigger, not smaller.

The Trait of Patience

Curiosity definitely plays a large role in creating a solid unschooling environment, but it's not the only factor. As we spend our days playing and digging into interests with our children, supporting them as they live and learn every day through a rainbow of emotions, there's another trait that will be called into play: patience.

Learning at Their Tempo

Finally! The first spring day to hit double-digit temperatures. You happily drive your daughter to the park to play. Amy runs around the playground for a few minutes but soon wants to walk in the nearby forest. "That's a great idea!" you exclaim as you both beeline for the path entrance. But ten minutes in you realize your progress has slowed to a snail's pace as

Amy bends over every few feet to examine yet another old leaf, or rock, or needle, or stick. Soon you just can't take another stop so you scoop Amy up into your arms and carry her back to the car.

Why is patience important for unschooling? Because it helps us parents move at our child's pace. Remember, we've chosen unschooling as the learning paradigm for our children and our family as the primary learning environment, so their learning is a big part of our days.

In the school environment, one of the challenges for teachers is that there is really only one pace at which they can move forward: that of the curriculum they need to cover in a fixed number of days. Some kids move faster, some slower, and the rate of learning is often not the same across the board, but dependent on the subject. Parents can fight for special services in an attempt to find a better match for their child's pace, but in a group environment it is very difficult to meet any one individual's needs specifically.

With unschooling we understand the value of the learning found in day-to-day living. So when our children are interested in something, we should, as best we can, slow down (or speed up, as the case may be) and meet them at *their* pace of discovery and exploration. With patience, you can help them dig into their learning as deeply as they are inspired, plus give them the time to absorb it at the pace that suits them best.

The more obvious academic topics can make practicing patience easier because we can quickly see the value of the learning happening in front of us. Their boundless curiosity as they dive into dinosaurs is such a beautiful sight to behold that answering their seemingly endless questions about the Jurassic Period can be more exciting than frustrating. And there's a bubbling joy to be found in watching the *Land Before Time* movies over and over, as well as quoting lines over dinner, acting out scenes in the yard, and setting up a prehistoric world in the living room, complete with your child's toy dinosaur collection. That joy reminds us to slow down and let them savour the moment; to allow them to fully immerse themselves in the experience.

The benefits of giving them the freedom to move at their own pace can be more obvious say, at the museum or science centre: they move happily from exhibit to exhibit, sometimes spending minutes, mere seconds, or an hour at each. I fondly remember many visits to our local science centre. Sometimes we only visited one or two exhibits during an entire afternoon, while other times we wandered through three whole floors in a couple hours. Each visit was interesting and fun in its own way, but they nicely illustrate how non-linear real learning can be. Any frustration I felt because I wanted to move faster than their pace was quite easily dissipated by remembering that their learning was my priority.

When I felt frustration rising as they ran ahead, I would take a moment to remind myself that I could spend more time at a particular exhibit next visit. Or, if they were still engaged as I lost interest, I would glance around for a nearby exhibit to catch my attention, or even choose to focus on watching their joy as they busily raised and lowered the hidden weights to change the water patterns in the tank so as to predict whether or not there was a nearby island or two long before there were GPSs for navigation. Years later I fondly remember that hour, glad that I was able to give them that breathing space to explore passionately until they were done. In contrast, the school kids visiting alongside us most typically had a fixed and relatively short amount of time at each exhibit, and they had no choice but to visit those on their teacher's list, regardless of interest. Much less enjoyment, and much less learning.

But there is also plenty of important learning that is less about the world and more about living in it: eating and sleeping and relationships and property and emotions and health and more. This knowledge is more focused on learning about themselves and how they relate to the world around them. Instead of straightforward facts, living is entangled with people and feelings and sensations and judgments so it can take longer to explore one's personality and how one relates with others, but it is definitely essential knowledge. And, as with all kinds of learning, exploring how they fit into the world works best when you meet and support them where they are and move at their pace.

We've been talking about patience in situations where parents get frustrated; now let's look at things from a slightly different perspective. What about when our children get frustrated with something they are doing? Our first reaction may be to try to get them to stop, "If you're frustrated, do something else for a while!" Their frustration frustrates us. Stopping may be a reasonable path forward, but it's not the only one available. Patience helps us step back a moment and see some of the other possibilities. And do you know what's often so fascinating about this situation—their level of commitment to accomplishing what they are trying to do. So much so that they are willing to be continually frustrated as they challenge themselves to keep trying.

Are we that persistent when we have a goal? How easily do we give up when we meet an obstacle that we can't quickly overcome? Reminding myself of this can help me shift from frustration at their persistence to seeing the beauty of their determination. From that perspective, I can empathize and more patiently help them find ways to move through the situation.

Whether it's putting on their shoes without help, or building a block tower as tall as they are, or beating the final boss in their video game, there's learning in everything they attempt. Whether they are learning the particular skill (tying their laces), or discovering where their limits are (does their skill diminish when they are frustrated?), or exploring the ways they can deal with frustration (does a break help? or a deep breath?), they are learning. When we recognize this, it helps us gather our patience and meet them where they are. We can help them to figure out both the task at hand, and the ways that work best for them to move forward when they find themselves frustrated. Maybe you can help by giving them small tips and encouragement (try using the bigger blocks at the bottom), or by sitting nearby as you research and share battle strategies from the internet, or by bringing a glass of water and a snack to share. By finding ways to help them, you show them other possibilities for moving through challenges beyond just expressing frustration.

There's a second reason why patience is really important: its positive effect on your relationships. Patience is a visible display of respect for, and understanding of, the child. You understand their determination when they want to try to use the spoon themselves, or attempt the monkey bars over and over until they get to the other side, or watch their favourite movie for the fifteenth time, or get to a good stopping point in their video game, or wish to have you wait at the studio during their dance class, or chat in detail about their thoughts, or take them here and there and back again. They are learning. They are living. In respecting their need to move and learn at their own pace, you undermine the conventional concept of adult power over children and they experience a concrete example of "we're in this together." This is a pretty significant shift from the paradigm where kids are expected to fit into their parent's needs and schedule, with the implication that the kids can get their way when they are grown up.

Annoyance Breaks Their Rhythm

Hmm, you haven't heard a peep from Henry for over an hour. Wondering what he's up to, you head down to the basement. Stepping around a heap of stuffed animals on the floor, you find him bent over the table sorting through the 500-piece puzzle he got last week

*at the thrift store. "Henry, come put away those stuffed
animals." Startled by the interruption he replies, "I'll
do it when I'm done." "No, do it now please," you say
firmly. Tearing himself away from the puzzle, he
huffs in frustration. "I was almost finished finding all
the edge pieces!" When you pass by a few minutes later
the stuffed animals are back in their bin but instead of
returning to his challenging puzzle, Henry is
watching repeats of his favourite TV show, his
comfort activity.*

Without patience, deep and connected learning is
compromised. Our impatience can often short-circuit our
child's learning by pulling their focus away from their
activity, and onto our frustration. Even if we change our
mind, they may not be able to get back into the flow of their
task at hand: their rhythm has been broken.

If they are engaged and you are getting frustrated, try
to extend their time by doing some thinking to get to the
root of your frustration. Is it with the activity itself? Or the
time it's taking? Do you have something else coming up
that's distracting you? Is it a firm commitment? If not, does
it really need to be met now?

Often, once you figure out the root of your frustration,
you can work through it without disturbing your children
at all. But, if you decide you do need to interject, at least
now you have a clearer understanding of why and can
explain it to them so there might be less frustration and
more understanding on their part about the intrusion.

When you find reasons to extend your patience, your children get to fully explore their Lego creations, enhancing their spatial skills as they try to create what they see in their mind, their small motor skills as they put together and take apart small pieces over and over, and their social skills as they play out elaborate scenarios with their creations. Nice! But maybe you don't have the patience for a Lego-strewn living room for days on end. I don't mean you need to swallow your frustration to support their learning. If something is truly frustrating for you or your spouse, or a sibling, work together to find a solution that allows them to explore to their heart's content, and enables others to meet their needs as well.

Perhaps you can find another room they can use, or maybe they can play on a big sheet or blanket that makes clean up easy. In our case, my husband built a big table with sides so that Lego pieces didn't often end up on the floor. The kids were happy too because their creations were at less risk of accidental damage from a stray step. And everyone's bare feet were happier. We reused plastic ice-cream containers to keep the pieces sorted—less mess that distracted my husband, and they found their pieces more easily. Times when they wanted me play with them longer than my imagination could muster, I could still sit with them and sort pieces and chat.

Without the time and space that a patient parent gifts a child, their learning may not be as deep and thorough as they might choose it to be. And it's patience in all the moments:

- patience for a messy bedroom, giving them the space to learn about themselves, about what their feelings toward clutter and organization are;
- patience for waiting as they chat with friends after karate class, honing their social skills and just plain having fun;
- patience for driving your children and their friends to each other's houses, to another activity in another city, where they continue to explore the world and their place in it; and
- patience to stay home another day, or week, or month, as they practice listening to themselves, exploring their thoughts, their anxieties, what brings them comfort.

How else might impatience hinder unschooling?

Expressing your impatience emotionally will not encourage long-term learning. Similar to when we interrupt their activity to move on to something else, snapping or yelling at them not only interrupts their learning, it also pushes their thoughts right out of their mind by immediately putting them on the defensive. And it can place an off-putting slant on the activity itself by connecting a negative memory to it. Recall how you felt when you were yelled at as a child. Chances are you remember being yelled at, but not much about the situation itself—that kind of emotional environment deeply interferes with any learning because at that point it becomes all about fear.

So if you feel the urge to yell to release your frustration, try to shift your focus from the emotion to the situation. Try to find other ways to recentre yourself when frustration grows: deep breaths, a short trip to the bathroom, trading off with a spouse or friend, a glass of water or cup of tea. Find tools that help *you* shift your focus from the emotion of impatience to the situation at hand. Do that first before moving forward with your child.

Practicing Patience

"Jennifer, time to leave!" When she doesn't reply you search her out. Finding her in her bedroom, still in her pyjamas, your frustration mounts. "The birthday party starts at 11am. We're going to be late if we don't leave in five minutes. Get dressed now!"

We've talked about some of the reasons why patience is important. It helps support your child's learning by meeting them where they are and moving forward at the speed they are comfortable with, and it gives you that moment to check that your interruptions don't subvert their learning unless truly necessary. It also supports your relationship by showing your understanding of, and respect for, where they are in that moment.

Understanding why patience is important is a great first step. Now let's talk about ways you can practice patience day-to-day.

Let's get some typical reasons for feeling impatient out of the way first. If you have a time commitment you're trying to meet, do a quick mental check of how important the commitment really is. Does Jennifer really need to be at the birthday party right when it starts? Maybe they are leaving as soon as everyone arrives to go to the park, so yes. Or maybe they are playing games in the backyard and arrival times are less critical.

Do you want to leave the park now to get home so you can cook dinner and have it ready by 6pm? Ask yourself if that's really so much a commitment you need to meet or a routine you may be stuck in. Or do you need to get out the door to a doctor's appointment? In other words, take a moment to ask yourself whether it is a need or a want. If it's a want, ask yourself why you want it, and whether it's worth this challenge to your relationship with your child. If it's a need and you find you and your child at odds, that's a clue to look for a different process next time a similar situation arises so you can move through it with more patience and grace.

Remember, transitions can be challenging for both children and adults. There are ways we can help our children move through them more gracefully. If they have trouble leaving the house you might bring a few of their loved things with them so the transition is less jarring; maybe add some stops to the trip that they would enjoy. Or if they find leaving places to go home challenging, have something interesting set up at home that they would look forward to like watching a new movie, starting a new craft, or playing a board game with you. Get to know them so well that you can not only anticipate their challenges but can also generate ways that will help them move through those challenges with less frustration. When you understand them that deeply, their actions are more logical and less frustrating, making patience much easier to find.

It can also help to have discussions about the plans beforehand so things aren't a surprise to them. Maybe right after breakfast that morning, Mom or Dad could have gone upstairs with Jennifer to help her pick out her birthday party outfit and to get dressed at a leisurely pace. If Jennifer often has a hard time with transitions that aren't routine, make the morning about enjoying the excitement of the upcoming party and getting ready with her.

Try out *their* ideas and suggestions about how to get ready and out the door in reasonable time. Maybe Jennifer asked if she could draw her own birthday card to bring, and that could be incorporated into the morning preparation activities. If it's been the topic for the morning, chances are getting out the door will be less stressful. It can also help to take a moment to talk about the outing afterward to see if there are any ideas to make the process more comfortable next time.

Beyond planning for times when you need to move others through your schedule, one thing I often do when I'm feeling impatient is to look at the situation from my child's perspective. That seemingly simple thing so often helps me understand why we are out-of-sync. What is it that they are thinking that calls them to move faster or slower than my pace right now? What is their goal in this moment and why do we find ourselves at cross-purposes?

Especially when my impatience is becoming a pattern, I want to figure the situation out. The first thing I do is look for clues. Your children's motivations, actions, and reactions will be based on the interplay of their unique personality and life experiences, so the same clues, or behaviours, can suggest different things for different people. Once you've gathered some clues about your child's behaviour and motivation, try to piece them together into a bigger picture—a view of what you might do to better support your child and take that understanding into your next interaction. And then do it all again—gather clues from that next interaction, think, and further develop your understanding, round and round.

Being able to analyze situations and see them from my child's perspective has been a key part of helping me develop patience, so I thought I'd work through an example to give you a better idea of what I mean. This is one of the short stories from my book, *Free to Learn*:

> *It's a beautiful fall day and you are looking forward to going for a walk. Jeremy quickly pulls on his running shoes, dashes out the door, and shouts, "Come on, Mom!" Your smile falters as you notice his sweater still hanging on the hook, remembering the talk you gave him just yesterday about wearing it when he goes out in this cooler weather. As you walk through the door you say firmly, "Jeremy, get back here and put on your sweater!" A beat passes and you add, "NOW!" Running back he protests that he's not cold, but you insist. He does as he's told but his excitement has waned and the joyful stroll you envisioned has morphed into a determined march around the block*

accompanied by repeated moans about the sweater,
and you both head back inside.

Why is this interaction one that might inspire the mom to dig into and learn from? Because somebody was unhappy. When *anybody* is unhappy with a situation it's worth taking the time to figure out why and what may be done differently in the future. In this case they were both frustrated and neither enjoyed the walk in the end.

Striving to understand your children deeply enough to anticipate their needs and frustrations as well as your own can go a long way to minimizing the frequency of situations that cause frustration. And the sooner you recognize the need for patience in a situation, the sooner you begin to move through this process.

So first, let's take a look at the scene from the Mom's perspective. What clues do we have that point to the thoughts and motivations behind her actions?

- She wants to enjoy a walk outside: It's a beautiful fall day and she's expecting Jeremy will enjoy going for a walk with her (she's smiling at the thought, and he's happily calling to her to get the activity started).

- She is adamant that Jeremy wear a sweater outside: Not only does she ask him to wear a sweater, she's insistent when they leave the house, and also throughout the walk.

From her perspective, I imagine it seems like a reasonable request (or she wouldn't be so insistent). It's cold outside, and she feels more comfortable in a sweater so it makes sense to her that Jeremy will too. She probably extrapolates the colder weather into imagining Jeremy sick with a cold and the challenges that can pose, so she wants to take any reasonable actions she can to prevent that outcome. Besides, wearing a sweater does not impede Jeremy's physical movements so she probably doesn't see an issue at all. She might think that, as his parent, Jeremy should trust her implicitly. He should know her actions are motivated by love, whether or not he understands her detailed motivation for insisting he wear a sweater. She probably wants him to learn that when it's cold outside he must wear warmer clothes. And maybe she feels that changing her mind once the activity has started would show weakness and encourage Jeremy to argue with her in the future. It's all rather logical, from her point of view.

Now let's look at the interaction from Jeremy's perspective and find clues that might point to how he interprets the situation.

- Jeremy wants to enjoy a walk outside: You can tell he's excited about the activity because he gets ready and out the door quickly, and calls for his mom to join him.
- Jeremy does not want to wear a sweater: He leaves the house without it, he hesitates to return when asked, and he complains about it throughout the walk.

So, from Jeremy's perspective, looking at the situation through his eyes, what might these clues tell us?

We know he's happy at the thought of spending time with his mom, of walking around the block. Once she insists he wear a sweater though, his mood changes. His actions suggest that he's just as sure as she is that the opposite is true: he'll be uncomfortably hot wearing the sweater during the walk. If he wasn't quite sure, he probably wouldn't be so insistent. He'd grab the sweater and be on his way. His insistence means it's an important point to him. Maybe it's another clue in a larger pattern of ongoing power struggles between them, pointing to bigger issues. Or maybe he's just frustrated his mom hasn't realized he's always feeling hot. In that instance, he probably feels like his mom is ignoring his real needs and doesn't think he can take care of himself. That she's spouting rules without taking the time to consider his perspective. It's another example, to him, that she doesn't really care about him. Looking through Jeremy's eyes, his thoughts and reactions are understandable as well!

After you have analyzed the situation, picked out the clues, and hypothesized how your child probably interpreted the situation, ask yourself, "Is that what you wanted them to learn from the situation?" It's so easy for the parent to think they are teaching one thing, (cold outside temperatures means wear warmer clothes) while the child is learning something completely different (mom doesn't consider my needs and thinks I can't take care of myself). Looking at a situation through the child's eyes gives us a chance to not only better understand our child's needs, but to also understand how they are interpreting the messages we are sending them through our actions. When the messages we want to send them and the messages they seem to receive are different, it's time to figure out why and to start trying to communicate more effectively, i.e., act in ways that better deliver the messages we intend.

So, in this hypothetical situation, how might Jeremy's mom take this new understanding and better communicate next time? Once she realizes, through her son's resistance to wearing a sweater, that this is important to him, even if she doesn't understand why, she can be patient and support his learning by dropping her own insistence. Immediately the power struggle is avoided and the situation is no longer about their relationship (who can insist longer, who has the power to control whom) and more about the son's real physical needs–and that's what the mom likely wanted him to learn about in the first place, how to take care of his physical needs.

And to support his learning even further, she can bring the sweater along. That gives him the opportunity to choose to put it on during the walk if he gets uncomfortably cold. Knowing the sweater is available, he is continuously choosing whether or not to put it on during their walk. He gains experience and learns more about what his mom really meant for him to learn—how to take care of his physical needs. The result? They are both physically comfortable and enjoy the walk, adding another happy and connecting experience.

Taking the time to see things through your child's eyes is not about giving up your perspective. It's a way to practice patience: don't jump to frustration before you better understand the situation and your child. It also improves your communication with them, building a more strongly connected and trusting relationship, things we'll talk about in later chapters.

And last, but not least, consider how *your* physical state impacts your ability to practice patience. Are you tired? Hungry? Thirsty? In need of some active movement? It's different for everyone, but figuring out and taking care of those needs will also go a long way to helping you practice patience. And don't forget to share what you're learning about yourself with your kids! "I'm sorry I'm getting cranky, I think I need to grab a snack because I'm getting hungry." "I'm feeling antsy and frustrated. I'm going to go run around the back yard for a few minutes. Anyone want to play tag?" Help your children discover how their body's physical needs and their mind's behaviour are connected.

Think about patience in your own life. Do you see benefits to both your children's exploration and learning and your relationship with them in those times where you have been able to be patient and move forward at their pace, finding the flow? Is there any commonality to the situations where you find patience hard to come by? Can you set up those situations differently in the future so patience is easier to reach for? Do you find even just the act of recognizing your frustration lessens it a bit? These are just some of the many ways to dig into learning more about patience and how you can use it to support learning and relationships in your unique family.

Patience Doesn't Mean Carte Blanche

"I'm going down the slide!" Landon shouts as he peels off toward the playground. You smile and start to walk in that direction. A dozen steps away, you hesitate as you see him push his way to the front of the line. Throwing the nearby parents an apologetic eye as you pass them, you meet Landon at the bottom of the slide. "Come push me on the swing!" he shouts as he runs for the open swing, just beating the younger child who was walking in that direction. After a few minutes of pushing him, you tell him it's time to leave to pick up his sister for dance class, but he ignores you as he rushes to the teeter-totter.

I do want to mention: patience is an area where not taking the time to understand the *why* behind it can come back to haunt newer unschoolers, like in the scenario above. Understanding the principles of unschooling *before* talking about the helpful characteristics that support it is important. That's why I didn't write this book first. In my experience, newer unschoolers sometimes hear things like "be patient" and "say yes," quick phrases that get to the point but not the underlying principles, and interpret them as rules of unschooling. Rules that, without understanding, can seem to imply you should give your children carte blanche—free rein to do whatever they please, whenever they feel like it.

Does that sound familiar? Determined to be great unschoolers, the parents vow to themselves that they will follow these rules no matter what comes up. They have amazing resolve, which is a great show of love for their family, but they are bound to burn out sooner or later. Why? Because it's the understanding of the underlying principles you bring to a situation that will inform your answers and questions and conversations with your children and in turn bring the most learning for them, and a better relationship with them.

If parents indiscriminately implement say yes, repeatedly reminding themselves to be patient with whatever happens as a result, the experience the children will be living is that they ask and they receive, end of story. And they learn what they live. They will begin to expect to always have their way, regardless of the situation, regardless of the people involved, and eventually the parents, even with their best effort at observing what they initially saw as the "rules" of unschooling success, will crash and burn and blame unschooling for the dreadful mess they find their family in. If you find yourself in a situation similar to Landon's parents, beating yourself up won't help, but do step back and start really learning about unschooling.

Moving to unschooling is a beautiful and challenging dance, a process. It's the give-and-take between seeing the beauty and potential of unschooling and excitedly wanting to jump right in, and realizing unschooling is a deep and marvellous subject and your family, ought to feel safe, loved, and supported during the journey. It's not a race.

On the flip side, don't dillydally about it—the benefits to your family are many. If you choose to start the journey, keep going. Keep learning about unschooling, keep learning deeply about the wonderful individuals in your family, and keep moving forward.

And realize that the journey of understanding unschooling doesn't end. I understand it more deeply as my kids get older and new situations present themselves. When my eldest turned sixteen, I had never unschooled a sixteen year-old before! I continue to figure out more each time I contemplate my kids' perspectives and choices, and experience moments of insight while observing other parents in action and their kids' resulting behaviour and actions. In choosing unschooling with your family, you have intentionally taken on a wonderful and important responsibility. Dive in attentively and enjoy!

The Power of Strong Relationships

The third common characteristic I've found in solid unschooling environments is a strong relationship between parent and child. The development and maintenance of a strong connection between parents and children is fundamental to unschooling because it promotes a peaceful atmosphere where both parents and children are comfortable approaching each other for candid discussions. Just as the relationship with a teacher can make or break the year for a child in school, your relationship with your child is crucial to their learning—this is where the rubber meets the road, so to speak. It's where you interact and connect with your child. It's living and learning together.

Building Relationships Connections

Family reunion time! You're actually pretty excited to see everyone; it's been a year. After you and your daughter drop the casserole dish in the kitchen, you turn around and there's Aunt Josie, ready to chat. "Is this your Penelope? She's grown so much!" Turning to Penelope, she asks "Do you still like video games?" Penelope nods and smiles and changes the subject. "Oh! I see Amy! I'm going to go say hi. Nice to see you, Aunt Josie." You smile and continue the conversation in her stead, "Yes, Penelope has been learning a lot about video game programming this year, and is working on her own game." Aunt Josie doesn't seem to listen as she soldiers on, "Aren't you worried about her being involved with all that violence?" It's the same question she's asked for years.

You can envision relationship connections as being similar to learning connections. What do I mean? Real learning is learning that is understood and remembered. And what helps someone understand something and remember it? Connecting it to something they already understand and remember. A new piece of knowledge that clicks like a puzzle piece slipping into place does so because it connects with something else and now the whole picture makes a bit more sense. That sense, that bit of deeper understanding, helps the learner remember it. Random factoids of information are often soon forgotten because they have no real connection to something they already know or are interested in knowing more about. If I visualize the connected bits and pieces of learning that one might do while digging into an interest, it resembles a web. Not one with an orderly, repetitive pattern, but one unique to the spinner, the learner; one that represents their personal learning and view of the world.

Let's dig into that a bit more. Seeing the many ways things relate to other things allows us to understand them more deeply. For example, photography is a quite a popular hobby. Many people find it appealing to document both the ordinary and the special moments of life in pictures. Yet if a child wants to dig deeper, it can be a window to the world. They may:

- discover new styles of art and techniques as they delve into their favourite photographers, sparking new ideas;
- come across written critiques and discussions about personal style which inspire them to explore their own unique style;
- dive extensively into learning about image manipulation techniques as they try to bring what they see in their imagination to life;
- become interested in images they find everywhere, not just in photography magazines, but also in fashion and geography and advertising and documentaries: we are surrounded by images.

There are a myriad of ways that learning can branch out from an interest in photography. And with each new connection, not only do they learn about that new topic, say fine art, but the knowledge also enhances their understanding of photography itself, expanding their personal view of the world.

Now let's look at how we can relate that process to learning about people.

There are strong parallels between learning connections and relationship connections at their core; they are about understanding things and understanding people. Seeing the many ways things relate to other things allows us to understand them more deeply. And seeing the many ways we can relate to other people allows us to understand them more deeply.

Let's look at the learning connections we talked about from a relationship perspective. For example, let's use my eldest son, Joseph, as the starting point in this analogy, as photography was. Now from the time he was young, I've known he likes video games. That's one relationship connection. Knowing that, I, or anyone else who's interested, can connect and converse with him through that topic. But that's pretty superficial. Being with him while he played and enjoying conversations with him about games showed me that he wasn't particularly interested in all video games, but role-playing games in particular—another connection. And soon I discovered that it's not just the role-playing games themselves, but the detailed stories they often tell—another connection. The more connections I make with him, the more I learn about him, and the better I know and understand him. And the better I know him, the stronger I can make these connections by relating to him through those threads: I can talk stories in general with him; I can let him know about that new role-playing video game I came across; I can discuss the impact of video games in general in our culture. As I delve deeper and strengthen each of these different connections, the deeper and stronger our relationship becomes. I don't just know him superficially; I see a bigger, more connected view of him as a whole being.

The more connections you build with your child, the better you understand them, and the stronger your relationship is. As one connection fades—maybe they are no longer as keenly interested in Harry Potter as they once were—you still have other connections going strong. And you continue to find new ways to connect as they develop new interests. Relationships are like living entities, always shifting, with some connections fading as others grow.

How Strong Relationships Support Real Learning

Jesse is riding his bike around his driveway, enjoying the bright fall day. His mind is busy. "How does a bike work?" You look up from your raking and chuckle. "Really? You're riding one, why don't you just watch what it does? The chain connects the gears attached to the back wheel and the pedals, so when you turn the pedals, the chain moves, turning the back wheel. Simple."

It makes sense that relationship connections are akin to learning connections, but why is a strong relationship important for learning? Understanding your children deeply and being able to see things from their perspective helps you better support them as they follow their interests and grow as a person. And that's how they learn.

In our story, I'm sure the parent didn't intend to belittle Jesse with their answer, yet I can imagine that he might be a little more wary of asking questions in the future because it's no fun to be laughed at. If that kind of attitude becomes typical, Jesse will probably avoid asking questions conversationally, instead censoring himself to ensure his questions are "good enough."

Yet learning often includes conversations. As thoughts swirl and ideas coalesce, questions are asked, answers are mulled over, and follow-up questions are proposed. A strong and trusting relationship is paramount because asking questions can be like baring your soul—they are a direct line to your thoughts, showing the other person where you're standing, metaphorically. When I ask a question, the person I'm asking knows what I'm thinking, leaving me feeling vulnerable (I may be opening myself up to ridicule and judgement).

It may not be as big an issue when kids are younger. The majority of their questions are fact based: they are learning about the world around them. "What is this?" "How do you do that?" You may not know the answer but half the fun is figuring it out together. With a strong relationship they trust you to help them find the answer.

But as your children get older, questions and discussions start to veer more and more into the social, moral, and philosophical realms. And to ask deep and personal questions of someone, you really need to trust them, trust that they won't belittle your thoughts and ideas, trust they won't try to control you to fit their agenda through their answers, even subtly.

If communication and connection fail time after time, eventually the person won't attempt it anymore. This is true for any relationship: adult to child, adult to adult, child to child. A strong relationship has minimal barriers to communication, meaning both participants are reasonably comfortable asking questions, and answering them.

That doesn't mean the conversations themselves are necessarily comfortable—there are some rather uncomfortable topics out there to be discussed—but that both people are willing and trust each other enough to engage in a truthful conversation. And each honest and supportive conversation creates another connection or deepens an existing one.

Imagine yourself as a parent of an unschooling teen and ask yourself a few questions. Do you share your life experiences with them in hopes that they will avoid making those same choices that you now see as mistakes? Do you expect your child to always make choices you agree with? To always make choices you understand? Are you expecting unschooling to make your child "perfect"? It's hard to answer yes to any of those questions when they are phrased this way, isn't it? But as they get older, as the consequences of their choices become far-reaching, it can be so easy to fall back on rules and guilt or shame to try to control another person.

But attempting to exert control over another person eats away at the trust and connections, at the relationship you have built with your child over the years. Mainstream parenting says that's the consequence of being a "good" parent. That it is inevitable in the teen years that the relationship will become strained, but that they'll understand and be grateful when they get older.

But it isn't inevitable. When my kids were young, my goal with unschooling was to live a full and interesting life with them in a stimulating and supportive learning environment where they could follow their interests and learn to their heart's content—academically, personally, and socially. Younger unschoolers are learning about themselves, how their brains process information and emotions, how their personality acts and reacts, in essence, how they fit into the world as the unique person they are.

That hasn't changed now that they're older. Their interests have grown and changed, the kinds of things they are learning have changed, but my original goal hasn't. As they grow into teens they are intelligent, mature, knowledgeable, and lots of fun to be around, but learning doesn't stop. They continue to learn in new places and situations, with new people and with new responsibilities. Learning how they fit into the world as their unique teen selves. And I continue to learn: I am learning how to be a parent of teens. And all this learning happens most successfully when we have strong and connected relationships.

As I mentioned earlier, with teens, questions and conversations more often centre around topics of a more ambiguous nature, less defined as right/wrong, more focused on becoming *the person they want to be*. That's an important bit, the person they want to be. With your love and support, your trust and connection, you are a key piece in this process. And part of that is giving them the space to figure out how your thoughts, ideas, and values fit in with their developing views; don't try to force your moral code onto them by virtue of being their parent. Well, certainly you can try, we see instances of that all around us, but you know what I mean. Examples abound of parents trying to instill their personal belief and value systems into their children. And if the child isn't receptive, the parents often resort to rules and consequences, which can tear into the relationship and create a downward spiral that is hard to stop.

You may also discover as your child gets older that they begin to do more and more of their processing internally. Not only are they more comfortable doing it on their own because they've done it with you many times before, they may also want to challenge themselves to handle things on their own, to take on more responsibilities. Giving them the time and space to try figure things out on their own is such an important part of the learning experience, whether learning about things or about life. Don't take it personally; don't take it as a sign that you are drifting apart. Just be sure you're keeping the lines of communication open, the relationship strong, and the trust level high so that they are comfortable coming to you at any point in a situation.

If and when they do come to talk, keep in mind that just because things may have happened before this point doesn't mean they were specifically hiding them from you. Coming to you shouldn't be seen as an admission of guilt by any means. It means they've reached a point where they want some help, some feedback, or just a sympathetic ear. Remember, even as they do things on their own, it helps them to know that you'll be available to support them whenever they decide they need it.

Sometimes it can be disconcerting to come into a situation in the midstream. If your teen, or adult child, or spouse for that matter, comes to talk to you about a situation that has already progressed past your comfort zone, take a couple minutes, or more, whatever you need, to regroup before moving forward with them. But the key is to move forward from that point *together*. Listen openly. Ask non-judgmental questions to help you understand the situation as much as possible, to figure out their perspective and to understand what they are hoping to get from you. Commiseration? Discussion? Direction? What are they looking for?

As any tension is released and the situation is discussed further, definitely point out if and where you might have recommended a different course of action. Even though it's in the past now, they can add that information to their learning and it's experience they can use when making choices in the future. But try not to give in to the temptation to step in and take over. It's important to work through these situations together. That's how they really learn about themselves, truly understand how they got into the situation, analyze it, and now with your help, find their path forward. Or else what they learn is only how you would react in these situations. That is, unless they specifically ask you to take over for them—and at that point, still be sure to explain your thought processes and choices so they understand why you are making the choices you are.

Another reason it's important to work together is that as parents, we aren't perfect either. Each of us is doing our best in the moment, being open to other ways to proceed if the current ideas aren't working as we hoped. We are all learning every day, about ourselves, about each other, about the world we live in.

Challenges? Start With Our Own Behaviour

Vicky Bennison, an unschooling friend of mine with teens, hit the nail on the head with this gem, part of a wonderful mini-rant against a parenting Facebook meme going around:

> *"I have never had to hunt you down like a bloodhound, because you have always told me where you were going, and if you didn't I would question what in my own behaviour caused you to change yours."*

Our own behaviour is always the place to start. Why? Because *that* is what's under our control. If you find your teen isn't talking to you and things seem to be going awry, there is likely an interesting reason. If you think your child is specifically hiding things from you because they don't trust you, or your reaction, then work on the relationship;

build that trust again, build that connection stronger. Don't tell them to trust you, show them that they can.

Our behaviour is rooted in our perspective, how we see things. That is the place from which we act. Same for our children. They choose their actions based on their own perspective and motivations. With a strong relationship, power struggles aren't a factor and their choices aren't about me. I know they aren't choosing to do something with the express purpose of getting a reaction out of me—that's the relationship we've developed over the years. Their behaviour is the result of the choices they make for themselves, for their own reasons. If I'm feeling frustrated with their actions, the question for me to ask is "Why did they make that choice?"

One answer may be that they didn't realize how their actions would affect me, or others around them, and I can certainly share that information with them for next time. But not anticipating that their action might distress me is a far cry from acting on purpose to upset me or others. And that's the difference between a positive and negative perspective when interpreting the behaviour of others. In fact, I do my best to assume positive intent, or at least certainly neutral, when interacting with everyone. The world isn't out to get me.

Choosing to live an unschooling lifestyle with my family does not mean we are inoculated against life's hard knocks, that we never have sticky issues to deal with. Our lives are not easier, nor our issues any less dramatic than others. It's more that I don't decide that just because we are facing a challenge somehow I or my child or unschooling has "failed." I don't assume negative intent and then need to blame the outcome on something or someone to feel better. Because my goal with unschooling is for my kids to learn and develop into the person they want to become, there really is no failure—it's all living.

There is no benefit to assigning blame. Instead there is learning and growth as a person. And it's from this perspective that these challenging moments allow unschooling to truly shine because it guides us to be our best selves in each moment and work through the situations together. And we're all the more strongly connected for it in the end. Again, during these times strong relationships are so important because they give both parent and child room to process and share and figure things out together.

If an issue does arise, confrontation, unless it's an immediate and serious health concern, may well backfire, so consider it carefully. It's risky business. If they have been avoiding the conversation with you, they probably aren't ready to talk. You can certainly ask around the topic, but forcing a conversation may seem confrontational to them and starting a conversation from an adversarial standpoint makes it even more challenging. In the meantime, while working on your connection, let them know you're around if they'd like to talk. Not explicitly; if they aren't feeling connected to you, a statement like that can feel critical, implying, "I know you have something on your mind and you're wrong to not talk about it with me."

Instead, show your support through your actions. Be available whenever they want to chat, about anything. Their TV shows, their games, their friends—the safer topics where your connections are still relatively strong. In these times be sure to drop what you're doing and give them your full attention. Show them that you care about what they have to say. And be careful not to say anything that could be construed as demeaning. You want to make it clear to them through your actions that they can feel safe talking to you, about anything. Remember, that processing is where the rich learning lies, and the deepest connections.

The challenges parents have with teens are often in relation to the lines we draw around certain activities; the understandable worry we hold as our teens get involved in more adult activities with more serious consequences. I gave the photography example earlier and I know most of us are pretty comfortable seeing the many different directions learning can take when a child dives into an interest, the web of connections made as they explore a topic. Let's move forward a few years and explore the learning that might swirl around a more teen-related topic, like drinking.

It's a hot topic, with intense discussion surrounding themes such as drinking and driving, addiction, and teen drinking. Think of your spontaneous reaction to my mentioning it right now, your mind likely jumping to thoughts about teens getting wasted and making bad or unsafe decisions. Fear. But drinking is a socially accepted adult activity. And as our children grow into adulthood, it's reasonable that they may be interested in exploring it. As with all learning, it's about where they are coming from as they learn, what their motivation is.

Think about it from a teen's perspective. If they live in an environment with strict rules against drinking, to explore the topic they will have to rebel against their parents' wishes. This is an alienating position to be forced to take and means there are no openings for conversations with their parents because they have to hide their exploration. Or maybe their home is not actively strict, the parents accept that teen drinking happens, but in their effort to not appear complicit, the topic is banned and discussion is basically off-limits. Again, the teen is left to explore on their own, though in this case they can probably call for a ride in an emergency situation. Of course, there are always the families where the parents really just don't care to be involved much at all.

What kind of learning is happening in these situations? The kids are interested, they want to explore the topic, but the only experience being shared and learned from here is the direct experience of the teen, and maybe their immediate peers. That's pretty limited. You might add in the conflicting advertising they've been exposed to over the years: the heart-wrenching ads depicting the drastic consequences of drinking and driving, versus the "your life will be awesome like mine when you drink" ads of the beer and liquor companies. All with seeds of truth but spun to the extreme ends of the spectrum in an ever-spiralling attempt to shout over each other. Fear versus fun. And that fear, while teens understand rationally that those outcomes are possible, feels very disconnected from their everyday lives. "That won't happen to me." That's why fear isn't a good motivator—people don't want to live in fear. It can be stressful and debilitating so they tend to ignore it rather than make the effort to interpret it realistically and incorporate it into their daily lives.

But what might things look like in a family where no topic is taboo? In these families, all sorts of things might come up in connection with drinking alcohol. Chances are the teens have probably already enjoyed some drinks along with their parents over the years as their curiosity was piqued: champagne on New Year's, wine with celebratory dinners, a cold beer on a hot summer afternoon. Or maybe alcohol just hasn't been part of the family's lifestyle, but the topic is not taboo either. If and when teens are interested in exploring it, sharing your experiences will help them learn more from a trusted source.

There are so many facets that might come up in conversation, from the range of physical and emotional effects of alcohol, to various motivations for drinking, to the risks of drinking and driving, to the idea of alcohol as a social lubricant, to the more factual side of things like how it's made, the history, the social conventions surrounding it, the nitty-gritty of how the body processes it and so on. There's also the topic of teen drinking itself and its place in society as a symbol of rebellion against parental rules, its misuse as a means to escape an unhappy life, as well as the topics of addiction and alcoholism, and related genetics. Better to give your teen good information so they can use it to make choices they are comfortable with.

Alcohol has had a profound effect on some lives, and it can be really hard to work through those fears to support the learning of the next generation. I don't mean working through them with a goal of getting past and ignoring them, but to be able to share your experience with your teen without being overwhelmed by those fears. Fear gets in the way of understanding, of real learning. And understanding is a much better place from which to make choices.

From the teen's perspective, which kind of family would feel most supportive of them as a growing and learning person? From the parent's perspective, in which kind of family do you think you would have the most significant input regarding the teen's learning about alcohol? If as a parent you choose to draw a line around any topic, you are in effect saying you don't want to be involved with their learning on that topic, if they choose to explore it. Remember, at the end of the day, you can't control another person's actions. They are going to make their own choices; they are going to explore things that they find interesting, things they come across in life.

If you want to best support their learning, at all ages, be open and involved. To that end, a strong relationship helps you to understand them as best you can, and provides support that helps them make choices that move them toward being the person they want to be, from where they are in this moment. Barring extenuating circumstances, teens don't want to make choices that hurt themselves. Yet in the media, and in conversation with acquaintances, we are bombarded with images of teens making "bad" choices.

At the karate dojo, all the kids show up for the same class. They all seem quite similar and it's not until you see them in action that you can begin to differentiate between them.

There's a wide range of motivations and perspectives. There are those that are there because a doctor recommended it based on an ADHD diagnosis; others because their parents want them to get some exercise; some are there because their parent insisted, even though they didn't feel like coming that particular night ("If I pay, you go."); and some that are there because they fully chose to be. After they bow in, they all behave according to their perspective, motivations, and personality. It's our actions that show who we are.

Same with teens showing up at a party: that act in itself shouldn't define them as "troublemakers" or "wild" or "rebels". Through what motivations are they acting? Are they there to escape controlling parents, their biggest motivation being to get out of their house? Is their goal to get drunk, act crazy, and finally get some attention this week? To drink enough to forget the pressure they feel in the rest of their life because they know no other ways to handle it? To have a couple drinks and relax and chat with their friends? To let loose and dance? To work up the courage to chat with the girl in the corner they like? So many perspectives. Not all are stereotypical teen partiers. In fact, when you look at them individually, maybe none are. They all have their stories. They are a collection of their experiences, perspectives, and personalities. Placing them in a box and judging them will not help any of them grow into the person they want to be.

In situations such as these, what often distinguishes an unschooling teen from their peers is simply the perspective and motivation with which they show up. One big difference is that most teens don't yet have a lot of experience analyzing situations and making choices—up to this point, their parents have probably been telling them what to do. Now they find themselves on their own in new situations and without any decision-making tools to help them make some reasonable assumptions and extrapolations. Not only that, they are also faced with competing motivations. They don't explicitly plan on ending up in a tight spot, but maybe their wish to escape the control of their parents is even stronger. That's really hard stuff to sort through on your own. They can end up making choices based more on going *against* someone else, rather than *for* themselves.

Conversely, an unschooling teen won't likely attempt things far out of their comfort zone because they don't feel controlled by others so there is no gnawing drive to escape. With freedom, they grow into these situations and choices when they feel ready to challenge themselves, at a wide range of ages—though it's not necessarily when you feel ready to let them go. And there will be choices made that, in the end, they wouldn't make again. More learning.

That's why having the patience to slow down and move at your child's pace while they analyze situations and make choices as they grow up is so important—that ability is essential to have in their toolbox, not only as teens, but as adults too.

If you don't yet have teens, this discussion might leave you feeling a bit overwhelmed. But remember, you will grow as a parent as your child grows. When your child is seven, don't challenge yourself to be the parent of a seventeen-year-old! Bear in mind that you will grow along with them; that your relationship will grow alongside both of you. For today, think "Wow. It'll be so fun to discover the parent I'll be when I have teens."

Also realize that it won't be as hard as you may imagine because you'll have spent those intervening years learning more and more about your children as people. Things they want, or don't want to do in the future will develop over time, and will be connected back to earlier interests and ideas. There really won't be too many big surprises.

For now, continue to grow with your child. Enjoy being challenged around your edges—from taking that extra outing this week because your child wants to go, to making that overnight trip to another city to see a show, to entertaining the possibility that your child may be moving out to explore life's adventures earlier than you expect.

If you stay open and supportive, if your relationship is strong and connected, if instead of seeing lines your child may not cross, you instead see your *child*, you will truly enjoy travelling through life together.

Cultivating Trust

We've discussed why curiosity and patience are really helpful traits for parents who choose unschooling, and how the development of strong relationships with their children not only creates long-lasting and fulfilling relationships, but also supports real and deep learning. Now let's turn our attention to the fourth characteristic of a thriving unschooling environment: trust.

Trust is a reasonably confident expectation of outcome, coupled with the courage to live with the ever-present fear of the unknown. It's not about trying to disregard our fears and pretend to be comfortable living with uncertainty. Instead, we can acknowledge our fears and find ways to build our trust to offset them. Trust and fear seem to live together on a continuum: the more you trust, the less you fear. As one grows, the other shrinks.

For me, trust is about projecting the confidence in unschooling I have developed through past events into the uncertainty of the future. It's human nature to want to reduce uncertainty in our lives because uncertainty generates fear, and fear is an uncomfortable place to live. Understanding that trust replaces fear, I focus on building my trust, on developing that confidence both in unschooling and in my children from past experiences and using it to create a reasonably confident expectation of the outcome of future events. The more confidence I have through past experience, the more trust I have moving forward.

One important thing to note is that the reasonably confident expectation of the outcome is not an expectation of *what* exactly that outcome will be, but that the outcome will likely fall within an expected range of reasonable results. It's very unlikely that it will come out of left field. Whether or not it is the desired result, there is still learning.

Trust is the Backbone of Unschooling

"Can I go see a movie with Kayla?"

"Sure. Her mom's going to go with you, right?"

"No, she's going to drop us off and pick us up after."

"Oh, that's not going to work. You need to go with an adult."

"But we'll be in a theatre full of people!"

"I said no, end of discussion."

In school, relationships are not built on trust, there are too many people involved for that to be feasible. Instead, there are rules that control the children's time and behaviour, curricula that control their learning paths, and tests that measure their progress. But as we've discussed before, that comprehensive control often comes at a cost: many students develop a deep aversion to learning in general that can take years to overcome. Not to mention absorbing the misconception that learning only happens in classrooms, which can stunt their learning as adults.

In contrast, developing a trusting relationship with our children is the backbone of unschooling because it supports *all* the things we are trying to accomplish:

- with curiosity, trust helps parents feel comfortable giving their children more leeway in pursuing their interests;
- with patience, trust helps parents feel comfortable giving their children more time to accomplish their actions; and
- with strong relationships, trust helps parents more quickly work through their fear in challenging situations. (Fear is not a good place from which to make choices as it can close many doors to learning, like the movie story we opened with.)

The development of this deep level of trust helps parents gain a level of confidence about the future that makes them feel comfortable moving forward each day, along with a measure of courage to deal with any fear as it arises. Without that trust, there is a level of uncertainty that many parents will find, understandably, too uncomfortable to sustain over the long run. Of course, the cost of developing relationships based in trust is time—it doesn't happen overnight. Control is implemented more quickly, but it also can quite easily damage the relationship.

How can you develop this trust? One way is through understanding. While living and learning with your children, continue to deepen your understanding of unschooling so that you will be able to make connections between the philosophy and what you observe in your family each day.

There are many ways you can expand your understanding of unschooling: reading books, blogs, newsletters, and websites; attending conferences to hear speakers and meet others at all points in the journey; meeting up with local home or unschooling groups to see other families in action and share personal experiences; and through observing your own children and making thoughtful connections and extrapolations based on your ideas about, and experiences with, learning.

Make a mental note of those times when you know in your soul that this lifestyle is really working well. Those mental notes help you gain understanding, confidence, and ultimately build trust in the process of unschooling, and in your children. The deepest trust happens when you see it in action for yourself, when your *understanding* meshes with your *experiences.*

Then when challenges arise, and they will, you have quick access to a huge net of good experiences that remind you that this is just a moment, not the end of the world. It's easy to forget about all those good moments when you are immersed in fear. Remember last week when you trusted. That helps you remember the whole person your child is; that they are not defined by the worry or fear that threatens to overwhelm you in this moment.

Lack of Trust Leads to Control

As you pass through the living room you notice John sprawled on the couch. "Are you still watching TV? Your brain will turn to mush! It's nice outside, turn the TV off and go out and play!"

As I mentioned earlier, without trust in both the process and your children, there is a level of uncertainty with unschooling that many parents will find too uncomfortable to live with. What happens if they commit to unschooling but then life rushes along and they don't take the time to be with their children, to observe unschooling in action? Without doing the work alongside their newly unschooling children to develop that deep level of understanding and trust, parents will probably find themselves frequently feeling uncomfortable and questioning unschooling, and themselves, "Why do they want to do the same thing all day?"; "Are they learning anything?"; "Why won't they stop nicely and come to the table when I call them to eat?"

That level of discomfort is just not sustainable over the long term. If, after a while, they don't understand what is happening and why, these parents will begin to feel the need to exert more control over their children's learning to relieve some of that stress. Yet philosophically we know that the best learning happens when our children are free to choose their learning paths, to follow their passions and interests at their own pace. When you are unschooling, that need to control is detrimental.

A parent who doesn't trust that their child is really learning much of value while playing video games is likely to surreptitiously control them by encouraging them to do something else, if not flat out putting constraints on their game time.

A parent who doesn't trust that their child is learning about reading by absorbing the literate world around them is likely to share unsolicited word pronunciations or ask their child to sound out words around them, if not flat out require fifteen minutes a day of reading exercises.

These actions may help the parents achieve a level of comfort day-to-day, but it is at the cost of their children's exploration and learning. And there's a good chance that this lack of trust will also damage their relationship because the children will feel judged and found wanting. They will feel like they aren't learning up to their parents' expectations. That in turn will discourage them from approaching their parents with questions and comments and conversation, which interferes with their learning. It becomes a downward spiral and self-fulfilling prophecy. Exerting control leads to the need for more control.

On a related note, children know when they are capable of more freedom and responsibility. Yet if their requests to say, walk on their own to the park down the street or sleep over at a friend's house, are consistently denied for no reason other than generalized fears, the children will begin to lose trust in their parents' judgement, Again, the overall relationship is damaged.

Instead, if you are worried that your child isn't learning much about reading, observe their day-to-day actions through that lens for a few weeks. Notice the words they recognize as they are playing video games, or browsing the TV guide, or cruising the aisles at the grocery store. Notice the words they are asking you to read for them. Notice how well they remember the stories you read to them. Learning to read is not a skill learned overnight; it is the process of pulling together many smaller skills, typically over a period of years. Yet your realization that they are reading can come seemingly out of the blue. Whenever you find yourself worried, or even just curious, about something, use this kind of analysis to dig into it further.

Building Trust Through Experience

Emily has always been wary of larger groups, and uncomfortable in new situations. She always wants you to stay with her, but she's six now and you think it's time she became more independent, so you signed her up for Girl Guides. "Emily, I know you'll love Brownies! There will be lots of other girls there and you'll play games and do crafts." She's not sure, but you manage to coax her to the first meeting. The other

*young girls are running around the gym, shouting
and laughing. As Emily stands there, almost frozen
with uncertainty, you take the opportunity to leave,
reasoning that she'll adjust faster if you aren't around.
Giving her a quick smile and wave goodbye, you say
brightly, "I'll be back when it's over. Have fun!"*

Your children don't trust you just because you are their
parent; they trust you because you have shown them that
you are worthy of their trust. You are showing them that
they can trust you by being available when they need
support, by showing your love consistently in words and
actions, and by helping them get *their* needs met. Not by
forcing them to conform to your wishes for their
behaviour.

Newer unschoolers often hear others say "trust your
kids," but it's not a switch you can turn on and off. Real,
deep trust builds with experience. At first you won't have
your own personal experience with unschooling to draw
on. To start, you can develop some trust in the experiences
shared by long-time unschoolers, in person or online. If the
description of their lives appeals to you, and their
suggestions make sense to you, you can choose to place
some trust in that and begin unschooling with your family.

That trust won't last forever though because your
family will begin to act according to their unique selves, so
your days won't look like those you've read about. To build
long-lasting trust, you need to absorb and process your own
day-to-day experiences, not gloss over them. Building trust
means regularly taking a moment to observe your children

in action and to think about how these experiences connect to each other over time. The afternoon they dug so deeply into that video game you were flabbergasted at their concentration. The evening they were hungry and helped themselves to a snack. The time they decided they wanted to rearrange their room and spent all day at it, determined to make their own nest just so. The day they made arrangements to see their friends, coming to you to okay their fully formed plans. The time they comforted their sibling, then invited them to join their game.

Remember and connect all those moments when things went well; when you saw unschooling in action, when you saw a compassionate and loving child in action. Commit to memory the flashes of learning you see as they are happily engaged in their activity, not to mention the learning about themselves you glimpse in the joys and sorrows they encounter each day. This is how you build your supportive net of memories that will, alongside your growing understanding about unschooling, help you through those times when your fear threatens to overwhelm your trust.

A caveat as you go about building trust: don't make the mistake of equating trust with leaving them alone. Don't use trust as an excuse to distance yourself. If you're meeting at the park with your local homeschooling group, don't use "I trust the kids to work it out" as an excuse to gather with the adults around the picnic table to chat and ignore the kids at play.

Often kids can use some adult help in navigating the social entanglements that can arise in group situations.

These are great skills to learn! How about showing them ways, through your example, of inviting new kids into their play? Of bouncing around ideas with others to create a unique version of tag that allows everyone interested to join in? Of ways for everyone to take turns with the badminton set you brought? Or bringing some board games or cards or colouring books as examples of ways to show consideration for those kids that may not enjoy more active park activities.

Gatherings, certainly those whose purpose is to bring children together socially, flow so much more smoothly when the kids' comfort and enjoyment has been thoughtfully considered. Everyone wins when the adults take the time to support the kids, rather than brushing off their needs under the guise of trust.

What about those times when issues or requests seem to appear out of the blue? Remind yourself that when they approach you, they have already decided that's their best course of action at this point, so see how it goes! Trust and help. Don't leave them to fend for themselves, don't be spiteful, don't start a running quiz of "what about this?" and "what about that?" Chances are they've already asked themselves these questions.

For example, Michael, my youngest, does not typically process things through conversation; he thinks them through on his own first, so I am less likely to immediately understand his motivations. He's busily pursuing his interests, and when he does come to me, I know he has his reasons and goals; I just don't yet know what they are. By trusting and respecting him, by meeting him where he is—

even when he's ahead of me—and helping him move forward as best I can, I don't slow down or derail his learning process. Instead of asking that he stop and catch me up first, I jump right in, trusting that he has a purpose and that I'll figure it out as the bigger picture emerges over time.

It's a very different process than his siblings, but I've found it's really fun to do things this way as well! From small things, like asking the location of an obscure piece of computer hardware that we haven't touched in six months, to larger ones, like buying tickets to a show by a band he hasn't yet mentioned to me, helping him stay in the flow of *his* learning is very satisfying.

Here's a longer story about the trust and respect my daughter and I share, as well as how it grows. When I wrote this, my daughter, having recently turned eighteen, had told me a few months earlier that she wanted to spend the summer in New York City pursuing her passion for photography. An eighteen-year-old Canadian living alone in that infamous city? My first thought was "crazy!" but I quickly realized it was based on generalized feelings of fear, which in turn were based on stereotypical knowledge; not solid reasons why it wouldn't work. I also realized I didn't know all the thinking and processing she'd done up to the point when she decided to share her dream. So instead of immediately throwing cold water on the idea by venting my fear, I chose to share her excitement at the idea and learn more.

Over the next few months she shared her motivations and her plans, in bits and pieces of conversation, both longer and in passing. Many of my concerns came up because she'd already thought of them and she had back up plans to address them. My trust grew. Doing my own work, I recalled previous trips she'd made on her own and how well she'd handled herself, her resourcefulness, her ability to think things through. My trust grew some more. And by me not waving it off as an outrageous plan and instead talking about the possibilities, her trust in me grew. We could converse honestly and openly, me raising concerns as I thought of them so we could work through them, her asking questions, knowing I'd not use them against her but try to help her find answers. It was a series of steps we were both taking. Our trust in each other grew.

And to ground myself, I remembered that being eighteen, she could up and go herself if she so chose—she didn't need my permission. With our strong relationship, that didn't even remotely come up in our conversations, but it was a reminder to me of how completely different our process was from what it could conceivably have been. As the time approached we were both quite comfortable with the plans, and the backup plans, and called on our courage and sense of adventure to move though the vague remaining discomfort of moving into a situation unfamiliar to both of us.

Now, I don't share this example to show that going to NYC alone is a good choice for any eighteen-year-old; our path is not "the answer." It was a great choice for Lissy because she really wanted to try it—not to escape from home, but to explore further afield. And her strong desire to go was in large part because she was ready to take this step. So we found a way to make it happen that we were both comfortable with. And bonus: she found an incredible community of artists gathered there, her learning skyrocketed, and her soul was bursting with joy. Yet even without that particular outcome it would have been a good learning experience because she also learned she could live on her own, she learned how to get settled in a new city, not to mention the ins and outs of moving and rent and money management and immigration.

But it definitely wouldn't be a good choice for everyone and that's why I always focus on discussing the process, not the answer. Each situation you encounter with your family will be unique because every person is unique. That's why understanding your family members, having strong relationships, and developing trust is so important. Not only do they help you make all those day-to-day choices and decisions, they are key to making these bigger decisions as well. And one other thing to note: if your child feels understood and respected, if they aren't feeling pressured to leave or nursing a drive to escape an oppressive home life, these bigger possibilities will remain exciting dreams talked about as future wishes until they are feeling reasonably comfortable that they are ready. Then at that point they'll move to making more solid plans.

Helping Older Children Build Trust in Unschooling

Jason was really looking forward to his first soccer practice of the season! Once everyone had arrived, the coach smiled and said "Hi, I'm Mr. White. Everybody take a turn introducing yourself and tell us where you go to school." He looked to the boy nearest him who started them off. Soon it was Jason's turn. "I'm Jason and I'm homeschooled." Some of the kids looked confused and later during the practice a few of them came up and asked how he learned stuff without a teacher. Jason shrugged it off, but at the next practice, one boy very earnestly explained "My mom says you'll never get into college if you don't go to school." Jason starts to wonder if that's true.

What if you have older children and your family has recently decided to give unschooling a try? They may be thrilled to stay home from school, but older children have absorbed more of the mainstream messages about education and learning and can be wary of this new approach once the initial excitement has passed. They might need more active support to develop some trust in the process. Maybe they had negative school experiences and now they actively avoid activities that remind them of school. Or their definition of learning is so wrapped up in what it looks like at school that anything else feels like slacking off to them. Either way, deschooling and exploring life will be helpful for them to relax and begin to see the learning found in living.

Joseph, my eldest, left school when he was nine, and he, and my daughter at seven, both avoided things that seemed schoolish, or had negative associations for them, for well over a year. For my daughter it was reading; for my son, writing (my youngest had only attended a few months of half-day junior kindergarten, so he had the least stuff to recover from). What helped was to let them choose when to stop, or forgo altogether, any activity without any judgment, even subtle non-verbal reactions, from me. And for me to be open and available to listen to their stories about school as they processed them. What kinds of things might you do to help them process their feelings and move forward?

"Ugh. I stopped playing my video game because the mini-game I'm at was just like those worksheets I hated doing over and over at school."

"Oh, that's so annoying. You'd think they could come up with something more interesting!"

From there you might brainstorm some ideas of your own ("maybe a puzzle instead of questions," "how about a mini-game where you are flown back to the beginning of the maze by a dragon each time you hit a dead end") and have a laugh, or, if they aren't the mood for that, you could suggest another activity: "Want to play Monopoly with me?" Or whatever they enjoy.

And if you find they sometimes worry about whether they are still learning, take the time to notice specific things they are picking up day-to-day. Not to use as "proof" in a big conversation about unschooling, but just to mention when a moment arises. Your goal is not to convince them, but to help them as they figure it out. If your child says they are worried they won't learn to read, you might reply brightly "I'm not worried. I've noticed that you're reading more of the TV guide on your own, and the signs at the grocery store." Or whatever examples are applicable in your lives. Then move on to something else.

I wouldn't try to explain or discuss unschooling with them at any length—giving the process that kind of power can actually take away from it. What I mean is, by giving unschooling specific learning goals such as reading, you take it beyond living fully in the moment. When even a small part of your, or their, mind is wondering about those goals (like them thinking, "Hmm, Mom says I'm learning math when I play Monopoly" while playing Monopoly) you can lose immersion in the moment—which is where the best learning is. I've found that kind of meta-thinking is best done by looking back on past activities: "Cool, I got faster at adding numbers together by playing Monopoly!"

Instead of worrying about the process (or worrying about their worry), just do. Throw yourselves into deschooling, into exploring all those things you've put off because you were tied to school's busy schedule. Have fun living life together! Enjoy things they love together, bring interesting things into their lives, and follow their lead. You'll learn so much about them, and they'll learn so much about themselves.

Eventually your trust reaches a point where you find you're rather comfortable even in those times when your children are pursuing interests and you don't yet understand why they find them appealing. You realize you don't feel the need to step in and redirect them. You now understand the process so much that you know that if you take the time to look deeply enough, you'll find their reasons, or that, if the value is not lasting, they'll move on to something else. You reach a point where you don't always have to know what they are getting out of something, to trust that they are. You are more and more comfortable with the unknown.

Remember, trust isn't about believing they'll make the same choices as you, but that they will make reasonable choices that make sense for *them*. The more you understand your children, appreciate their likes and dislikes, their environmental preferences, and their usual actions and reactions in both everyday situations and less common ones, the more understandable and predictable their choices will be. And the more predictable, the less you are dealing with the unknown, which lessens your fear and allows you to trust more.

And along those lines, understanding yourself is also incredibly helpful. As I've mentioned before, supporting your children is not about disregarding your feelings, but about working together to find a path forward with which everyone is reasonably comfortable. But if you don't understand yourself well, then you may end up being the one who cries wolf too many times—a person who is led more by their fears than by their awareness. If you have done the work to understand *why* you feel the way you do, you can articulate those feelings to your family in discussions so it is understood. And when it's understood, it can be accommodated. But if you regularly allow fear to rule your actions and reactions, they can seem to be excessive to others, eroding their trust in you as a reasonable person. With trust, on those rare occasions when you aren't able to articulate your feelings well, they will still happily accommodate you. As you would do for them.

The trust and respect for one another that shines brightly in experienced unschooling families is not only a beautiful thing to see in action, it also promises wonderful relationships throughout their lifetime.

Putting It All Together

In *Free to Live* we've talked about the key characteristics of a thriving unschooling home: curiosity, patience, strong relationships, and trust. Each characteristic is important enough to stand on its own, yet there are wonderful interrelationships between them, with each one supporting the others in various ways.

Curiosity encourages us to be patient because we really want to take the time to understand the world around us. That cushion of patience gives us the space to examine our own experiences and to explore the perspectives of our children, which in turn builds understanding, trust, and strong relationships. Strong relationships inspire us to understand our children even better, motivating us to be curious about their interests, to extend our patience beyond typical bounds, and to trust them when things seem murky. And trust invites us to dig with curiosity alongside our children into things that might not have caught our interest initially, to be patient with them as they figure things out at their own speed, and to have those experiences we might at first be fearful of that so often build strong relationships.

These characteristics, taken together, create a thriving unschooling home.

Why Comparisons Don't Work

As you're learning about unschooling, chances are you'll hear or read stories about other unschooling families. Often they sound lovely and it's tempting to wish your days looked like that. Chances are that at some point you'll wonder, maybe even worry, "How come our unschooling days don't look like theirs?"

To answer this, let's take a step back and see how all these pieces we've been discussing come together. The key is understanding how the characteristics of an unschooling home strongly support the principles of unschooling to create an effective learning environment and a joyful home. From there, parents can figure out how to best support their children's day-to-day living and learning within the unique combination of personalities that make up their family.

What's so great about that? With this deeper level of understanding parents no longer get sidetracked (at least for long, anyway) comparing themselves to some model of unschooling perfection because they now realize there is no such thing! There's no model of a "perfect" unschooling child or a "perfect" unschooling parent. Those seemingly "perfect" unschooling families are really just predominantly successful implementations of unschooling principles and characteristics sculpted to harmonize with the unique people in that family. The parents understand unschooling deeply enough to create a supportive day-to-day environment that allows living and learning to thrive.

So next time you hear or read about a lovely unschooling day remember that they are different people, and how *they* do things to lovingly support each other may well not work for you and your children. You may try to do the exact same things and end up with some very unhappy campers! If that happens, don't be tempted to blame the unschooling. Instead, use it as a cue to dig deeper into understanding your own inimitable children.

But it's still wonderful to hear stories about other unschooling families—they are inspiring and energizing. Just remember, their stories are not meant to be set in stone, rather, beautiful clues to the terrain that can help you map out your family's distinctive road to a joyful unschooling life together.

Exploring Unschooling

Making the choice to move to unschooling isn't a lifelong decision, though I would suggest giving it a solid year before moving on because the deschooling process can take that long. If people ask, you can say you're trying it out for now and will see how it goes for your family. But do your utmost not to interfere with the process during that time (for example, by directing or judging your children's learning) or it may take even longer.

And there's an additional consideration if your kids are already attending school: forcing them to stay home from school could add a strong layer of resentment that would need to be overcome for unschooling to blossom. When we started, my husband and I decided to give it a year and see where we stood, understanding the kids could always go back to school. And we asked the kids if they *wanted* to stay home.

After this year you may decide some things just doesn't mesh with your family, for whatever reasons. As I mentioned at the beginning, unschooling isn't for all parents. That's okay, there's no club giving out special awards for choosing unschooling as your children's learning environment. If at the end of your year of unschooling it just doesn't seem like a good fit for your family, keep looking. If, after understanding and experiencing the principles of unschooling, you don't fully agree and support them, you won't be able to commit to creating a thriving unschooling environment for your children. Continuing to unschool at that point would be a disservice to the whole family. Better to take your experiences and deeper understanding of learning and move forward, finding a learning environment that better fits your family.

A Snapshot of Life

Let's put it all together by looking at the possibilities contained in a snapshot of a family evening. Imagine you're tired. It's 11pm and you've had a long day. Your bed is calling to you. Suddenly, you hear your son exclaim, "Come see this!" You know he has been happily engaged watching YouTube videos for the last half an hour. What might you do?

Take stock of yourself in this moment, and of your son's day and his perspective. You know he's digging into something, being curious, learning. Ask yourself if you're curious about it too. Notice if that wakes you up enough to take a few more minutes in your day. If your son's been having a challenging day and he's sounding happy and relaxed now, can you summon the patience to take a few more minutes to go enjoy his company? Understanding the rewards of supporting his curiosity, the benefits to your relationship of showing some patience to stretch your day out a bit longer, as well as understanding how you feel in the moment, puts you in a better position to make a fully considered choice without resentment.

Whether or not you go to bed or spend a few minutes watching YouTube videos isn't really the point. This definitely isn't to belittle you if you choose to call it a day. But now you know why you made that choice. You understand the gift you have given yourself and appreciate it. Take a moment to go tell him that you're really tired and feeling cranky and you'd love to see it in the morning.

That's a number of pieces of information you're passing along to him. You're giving him another piece of the puzzle of you, you're showing him an example of a way to nicely say no that he can reference in the future, and last, but not least, you're letting him know that you considered the request, that your choice to go to bed wasn't random, and therefore has a sense of predictability for the future. Give him a kiss good night. Remember the moment.

If the situation does arise again, maybe you can give the gift to him. Not tit-for-tat, but evaluating each situation, each time. But if you find that you're gifting yourself more often than not, that may be a clue to evaluate the environment more closely to set yourself up for more success with others in your family.

Do your children stay up late often? Can you take a nap so you are more actively available when they are more likely to be reaching out to you? Can you proactively go to them during the day? "Hey, can you show me that YouTube video you mentioned last night?"

These are ideas, possibilities, none are right or wrong. The point is to figure out how unschooling will thrive in your unique family environment. It's a process, the process of living. It's life—an amazing, joyful life.

Thank you!

Thanks for inviting me along on your unschooling journey. I hope you've found this book a helpful part of your exploration of unschooling. I wish you and your family all the best as you continue to live and learn!

If you'd like to stay in touch, you're welcome to sign up for my newsletter online at:
livingjoyfully.ca/newsletter

When you sign up you'll also receive my *Exploring Unschooling* email series.

Learning freely, living joyfully.

Acknowledgements

I would like to profusely thank my lovely editor, Alex Peace. She makes the editing process almost as much fun as the writing process! It is such a pleasure working with her and any errors that still reside in the manuscript are my responsibility.

My greatest sources of inspiration are my children: Joseph, Lissy, and Michael. Looking to them when I begin to question, well, just about anything, always points me in the right direction. Thanks for being you.

A special thank you goes to Lissy for the wonderful pictures that grace the covers of both my "Free to" books. Expressed through her unique perspective, these images embody the joy, freedom, and childhood wonder that represent unschooling.

I'd also like to thank Sandra Dodd for reading an early draft of the manuscript and providing, as always, such helpful feedback.

And I am, as always, very grateful to Rocco Laricchia for his willingness to question the conventional education system alongside me and find the answers that worked best for our family.

Other Books by Pam Laricchia

Free to Learn: Five Ideas for a Joyful Unschooling Life

Pam shares the five paradigm-changing ideas about learning and living that freed her family from the school schedule: real learning, following interests, making choices, why not yes, and living together. These ideas were, and still are, key to our unschooling lives.

Life through the Lens of Unschooling: A Living Joyfully Companion

Drawn from her popular blog at livingjoyfully.ca, you'll find essays tackling everything from learning to read to visiting relatives, all organized around nine key words that have been woven into the fabric of their unschooling lives: deschooling, learning, days, parenting, relationships, family, lifestyle, unconventional, and perspective. Come dig deeper into your understanding of unschooling and what it might look like day-to-day in your family. The theme is life; the lens—unschooling.

Libre d'apprendre: Cinq idées pour vivre le unschooling dans la joie

French translation of *Free to Learn*, by Malika Kergoat and Édith Chabot-Laflamme.

Un mode de vie hors des murs et de la pensée de l'école.
Vous envisagez l'école à la maison ? Le unschooling vous intrigue ?
Suivez-moi, je partage ici avec vous cinq idées ayant pour thème l'apprentissage et la vie ; cinq changements de paradigme qui ont libéré ma famille du carcan scolaire. Au fil de plus de dix années d'expérience, j'ai vu ô combien ces idées étaient essentielles, et le sont toujours, dans nos vies de unschooling. Au travers d'histoires, d'exemples et d'un langage clair, Libre d'apprendre explore toute la profondeur et le potentiel du unschooling.

You can also find Pam online at livingjoyfully.ca.

Made in the USA
Monee, IL
14 August 2020

38476567R00059